CREATIVE CRAFTS

MOIRA BUTTERFIELD

CONTENTS

Happy Super 8th
We'll be expecting
lots of creative gifts =♡

love
Uncle Billy,
Aunt Sally &
Mackenzie

Getting started

IN THIS BOOK THERE ARE LOTS OF DIFFERENT crafts for you to try. Each section shows projects which are simple enough for beginners, and there are lots of suggestions for other ideas to experiment with. The projects have all been designed so that you can get good results quickly and cheaply.

▲ *A papier mache bowl makes a great gift for a special someone*

SUCCESSFUL CRAFTS

Before you choose which craft idea to make, think about who it is for and how it will be used.

If you are making something as a present for someone, think about the kind of taste they have: for instance, what style of clothes they wear and what ornaments they have in their home. If you follow their taste when you make something for them, your present is more likely to be a success.

If you are making something for yourself, use your favorite colors. You could even work your name or references to your hobbies into the design.

If you are making something to display in a particular room, think what color the room is, and then match or contrast the colors of the craft item you intend to make. You could adapt the design according to the activity in a particular room; for instance, you could use images of different foods for a kitchen object, and images of fish, boats, and mermaids for a bathroom object.

▲ *This snake is made by a method of fabric painting known as batik.*

cotton reels

CRAFT KIT

It's a good idea to start gathering together a basic craft kit which will be useful whichever project you try. You will need to buy some of the items, but you can collect the others over time.

• Buy a pencil, water-washable glue, clear tape, scissors, water-washable paints, a selection of paintbrushes, and a set of crayons. A sketchpad would be useful, too.
• For some of the crafts in this book you also need a small sewing kit, including pins, a needle, and some thread.

• Collect scrap paper and card, clean empty plastic pots and cartons, scrap fabric, wool, and catalogues.
• To store your craft kit, get a large empty cardboard box (you could find one in a supermarket). Decorate the box with paint or cut-out paper shapes.
• Buy a few special items for some crafts, such as fabric paints or cold-water dye.
• Before you start a craft, make sure you read the instructions for the product you buy.

CHOOSING A CRAFT

When you choose a craft to try, bear in mind how much time you have and how much money you want to spend to get the equipment and materials you need. For instance, if you want to complete a craft in a few hours, don't choose papier mache, which takes a few days to complete. If you don't want to buy any extra materials, try a

▲ *Designing your own wrapping paper makes a present really special.*

craft such as collage, using items you already have around the house.

Don't worry if you don't get the exact results shown in the book. Use the photographs of objects as guides to help you create your own original pieces.

Poster paints and paintbrush

Pins

Scissors

Craft planning

BEFORE YOU START A CRAFT IT IS important to plan your work carefully. Make rough sketches and color them in with crayons or felt-tip pens, so you have some idea of what the finished design will be.

Colored paper

DESIGN RESEARCH

You may find that there is something special that you want to draw or paint. For instance, you may want to make a design in the shape of an animal. In that case, go to the library and find a book that shows you the shape and colors you need. You could also put real objects in front of you, such as leaves and flowers, and copy what you see.

Many of the crafts in this book are traditional. Once you get interested in a particular method, go to the library and find books on craft techniques and design in history. Look out for inspiration in museums and art galleries, too.

DESIGNING IDEAS

Gather together pencils, crayons, an eraser, a ruler, some plain scrap paper or a sketchpad, and some tracing paper.

Draw three or four simple outlines of the object you want to make and then use crayons to get different effects. Don't worry about making your design look realistic. Instead, concentrate on the mix of colors you will use and the shapes you want to show. It is often best to keep the design simple. That way, the effect you want will be easier to achieve.

Eraser

Colored

Colored felt-tip pens

Stencil paper

Tracing paper

Sketching and tracing

When you are planning your work it may help if you look at references to copy or to inspire new ideas of your own. For instance, if you are fabric-painting a T-shirt you may want to find a photo or a magazine picture to copy. Trace the outline of the picture. Then cut out the traced shape and draw round it onto the fabric or the paper you are using for your craft.

Enlarging a design

You may find a reference picture that you want to enlarge to fit your craft object. Here's how:

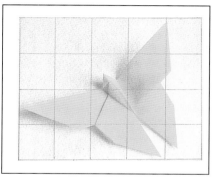

I First, draw a square grid over the picture. Use a ruler and pencil to do this, dividing it up into equal squares. If you don't want to draw directly onto the reference, tape tracing paper over it and draw your grid onto this.

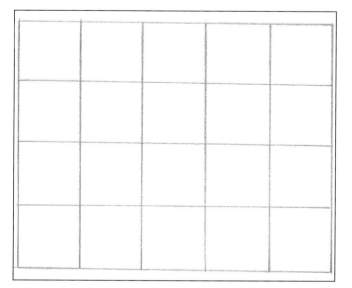

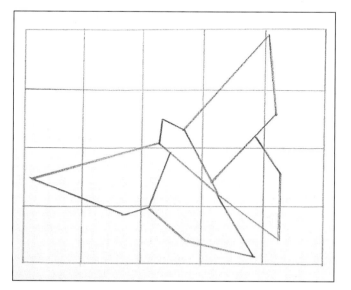

2 Decide roughly how big you want the picture to be (for instance, twice or three times as big as the original). Then, draw a larger grid on paper with the same number of squares, but that much bigger.

3 Using the first, smaller grid as a guide, copy the picture onto the larger grid you have made. Notice which parts of the picture fit into which square. The squares in the grid shown above are twice the size of the squares in the smaller grid.

Paper flowers

Paper and thin card can be cut and folded to make all kinds of clever-looking objects! Either use pre-colored paper, or paint onto it before or after you have made a model. Keep a collection of paper scraps in an envelope or folder so that you always have pieces to use. Start by practicing the basic techniques shown below.

Scoring card

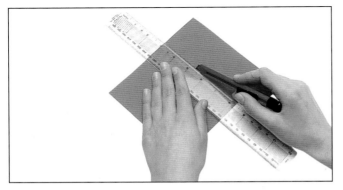

1 To make a neat fold in thin card, it is best to "score" the foldline first by laying a ruler along the line and "drawing" along the ruler edge with the blunt edge of a pair of scissors.

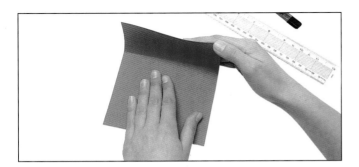

2 Fold the foldline, bending the card the opposite way to the scored line. It will fold with a neat, sharp edge.

Paper flowers

Use paper folding to make these pretty flowers. They will last much longer than the real thing, so they make an ideal present.

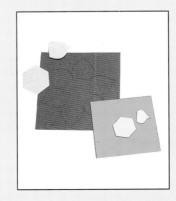

1 Cut out a six-sided template from one piece of card and a petal shape from another piece. Place the first template in the center of a piece of colored paper and draw round it. Place the petal template against each side in turn tracing round it each time to make a flower shape with equal-sized petals.

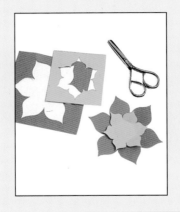

2 Make a smaller flower shape in the same way, using different-colored paper. Then, cut both flower shapes and glue the smaller shape onto the center of the larger one.

◄ *To make an unusual table decoration, try floating your favorite selection of paper flowers in a glass bowl filled with colored water.*

Put some paint or ink in the water to color it.

3 *Cut out a circle of paper for the center of the flower. Snip into the edge all the way around and bend the frayed edge upwards. Stick this onto the center of the flower with glue. Bend the petals upward to make the flower look more realistic.*

4 *You can make lots of flowers in this way, with different size and color petals and center. If you like, cut some leaves and glue them to the flower shapes. Make them long and spiky, or rounded and feathery.*

For stems use long, thin tubes of green card.

Cut out leaves and glue them to the inside top of the vase.

▲ *This paper vase is ideal for displaying your flowers. Make it by gluing strips of colored card around a toilet-roll tube. Then cut flaps at the top, fold and glue to the back of the flowers.*

Paper puppets

Make a mouse and some walking finger puppets decorated with folded and curled paper. Then make a little stage for them to perform on. They make good miniature presents, too.

Mouse Theatre

Put your finger in the back of this mouse to make it creep along. To curl the card for its head and body, put it under a ruler, and pull it upward in a curve.

Finger Mouse

1 Cut out a semicircle of pink paper and snip off one end. Cut a fringed strip of white paper with a red dot in the middle for the whiskers and nose. Cut out ears and eyes as shown.

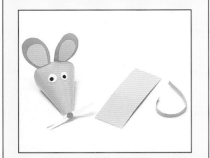

2 Fold the semicircle around and glue it to make a cone. Glue on the whiskers, eyes, and ears, as shown. Cut out a pink rectangle, fold it round, and glue it to make a body tube. Glue it behind the mouse's head and glue a curly tail to the back.

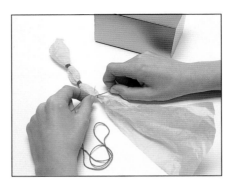

1 To transform a box into a stage, first paint it or cover it with paper. Then measure around the top and cut a slightly longer length of tissue paper. Tie thread around the paper at intervals, as shown, to make a row of tissue paper bunches. Fan out the paper a little between the threads.

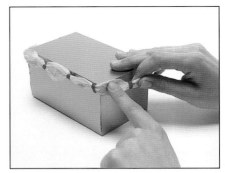

2 Use a thin paintbrush to dot glue onto the back of the pieces of thread along the tissue paper strip. Affix the strip to the outer top edge of the box for a theater stage decoration. You may need to do an edge at a time, making sure that it has stuck before going on to the next side.

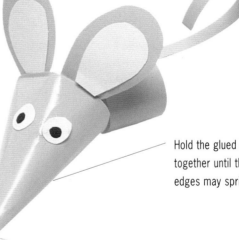

Hold the glued edges of the body and head together until they feel firm. Otherwise the edges may spring apart.

Here are some more ideas
for fun finger puppets.
You will be able to think
of many more!

▲ *Make your finger puppets dance on
top of the theater box. You could use two
at a time, one on each hand.*

The lightning is made from
card that has been scored
and folded.

Use a black disc of
card as a base for
this thundercloud.

Make a head and
some clothes, as
shown.

A paper tube that will fit two
fingers makes a puppet body.

two finger
holes

◀ *This funny snowflake
is made from a disc of
black card.*

9

Stenciling

STENCILING IS A QUICK WAY TO make things look as if they have been printed. By cutting out simple shapes from card and dabbing paint through the holes, you can "print" patterns repeatedly. Then you can decorate all kinds of objects, such as envelopes, writing paper, cards, paper tablecloths, and even three-dimensional objects, such as boxes.

PICTURE PATTERNS

A paper doily has pre-cut holes that make it ideal for stenciling patterns. Tape the doily on plain paper and dab different-colored paint over it.

Move the doily only when the paint is fully dry.

MAKING STENCILS TO USE ON PAPER OR CARD

Follow the steps below to stencil on paper. Cut the stencils on an old tray and then use bright paint to transfer the shapes to colored paper.

1 *Draw the shapes you want on card, spacing them out evenly for a clean, finished effect.*

2 *Cut the shapes out carefully with a craft knife. Then position the card on the paper.*

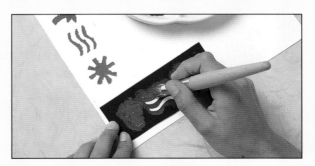

3 *Using a stubby brush or a sponge, dab thick paint through the holes. Then carefully lift the card.*

STENCILED STATIONERY

Here are some ideas for making stenciled stationery. You could stencil matching designs onto envelopes and writing paper to make your own personalized stationery set.

Stencil designs onto writing paper and envelopes to make a matching set.

Stencil round the edges of writing paper to make it look extra colorful.

Stencil party invitations with balloons or bows, or stencil a birthday card with the receiver's name.

Papier Mache

PAPIER MACHE MEANS "MASHED PAPER" IN FRENCH. THIS craft uses layers of paper which are soaked in glue and then stuck together to make attractive, usable objects. Papier mache has been used for centuries — it is surprisingly simple to make.

BALLOON BOWL

A papier mache bowl painted in bright patterns looks stunning. Paint the inside a different color.

1 Cover your work surface with newspaper. Tape half a toilet-roll tube to the top of a blown-up balloon to hold it above the work surface. Rub petroleum jelly over the balloon. Tear newspaper strips about 1in (2cm) x 1.5in (4 cm), and dip them into the bowl of wallpaper paste.

3 Trim off the rough edges of the bowl. Paint the inside and, when this is dry, the outside of the bowl. Finish with a coat of varnish.

▼ *Paint a picture on your papier mache bowl, as shown below, or dab paint onto a plain background with a clean sponge.*

Always wait for one paint layer to dry before you paint another on top of it.

2 Stick the gluey paper strips to the top half of the balloon, overlapping them to make a bowl-shaped layer. When you have built up five or six layers, put the balloon and bowl somewhere warm to dry. After a day or two, the papier mache will be dry and hard. Pop the balloon and gently peel it away from the inside of the bowl.

BALLOON VASE

This colorful vase is made from a long balloon using the same method as for the bowl. The decorative top is made by attaching a ring of card to the top of the balloon, which is then covered with papier mache.

To display flowers inside your papier mache vase, put a glass jar inside to hold the water.

Try scrunching up the papier mache a little to create unusual shapes.

PAPIER MACHE DISH

Clean polystyrene trays that form the backing for meat and vegetables can be recycled as a base for making your own imaginative dishes or trays. Build up five or six layers of papier mache on the front, back, and sides. Lay it on a sheet of polythene to dry.

A coat of varnish will keep the dish well protected.

Decoupage

THE WORD DECOUPAGE COMES from the French word *decouper*, meaning "to cut." Cut-out printed images are glued to the surface of an object to decorate it. With decoupage you can use paper pictures to alter an ordinary household object into something unique and beautiful!

WHAT YOU NEED

Small scissors
Pictures (from magazines, birthday cards, or wrapping paper)
Empty box
Paint
Glue
Clean cloth or sponge
Varnish

GIFT BOX

Transform an ordinary box into a stunning gift box. Decorate it with colorful pictures cut from birthday cards, wrapping paper, or magazines.

1 *Paint the box all over, inside and out, with a bright color. This will be the background for the decoupage.*

2 *Cut out your chosen pictures. It is best to choose pictures with clear outlines so that you have easy edges to cut around.*

3 *Decide where to place your pictures to make an overall pattern or design. Brush glue over the back of each picture and firmly press it into position. Wipe off any extra glue with a clean cloth or sponge. Leave to dry and then varnish.*

The objects on this "fishy" box overlap to give a three-dimensional effect!

PERFECT PLATES

Find a brightly colored paper plate. Stick on cut-out pictures from wrapping paper, either in the middle or around the outside, as a border. Varnish the plate and hang it on a wall.

Cut out a photograph of a pop star or sporting hero and stick it in the center of the plate. Surround the photo with cut-outs of suitable objects.

Think about the background color carefully before you start painting.

COLORFUL COOKIE TIN

Paint an empty cookie tin with latex paint. When the paint is thoroughly dry, stick decoupage shapes or objects over it. This one has been made using pictures from old-fashioned wrapping paper on a deep red background.

When positioning the decoupage cut-outs, remember you can allow some of the background color to show through as part of the design.

◀ *This heart-shaped brooch is made from card, with a safety-pin glued or taped on the back.*

Add decoupage, matching ribbons, and lace.

Simple batik

Batik is a method of fabric painting that is traditional in Asia. It produces brightly-colored patterns and shapes, usually with a white outline. Traditional batik is hard to do because it involves the use of hot wax. Here is an easy way to get the same effect using a mixture of flour and water.

What you need

White cotton fabric
(try starting with a simple square shape)
Fabric paints
Flour and water
Paint brushes
Old shirt, to protect clothes
Plastic bag, to protect any surfaces
Paper and crayons for doing
a rough design
Cleaned-out plastic squeeze bottle

Batik snake picture

1 Mix the flour and water to make a runny dough. Stretch out the fabric on top of a plastic bag. If you want, tape the edges down with masking tape. Unscrew the top of the plastic bottle and pour the flour and water mix into it through a funnel.

2 Screw the top back on the bottle and paint patterns with it, or outline a shape, on the fabric. Leave the dough to dry overnight. When dry, use fabric paints to cover in the areas inbetween the dough lines.

3 When the paint has dried, pick off the dough with your fingers and watch your batik design emerge. You will find that the fabric under the dough has stayed white. Fix the paint colors using the manufacturer's instructions.

◀ Here's the finished snake picture. You could try patterns instead of a picture, or even random shapes, on your fabric. Your mistakes usually just add to the originality of your work!

Wild designs, such as this, could enliven a cushion cover or a T-shirt.

Friendship bracelets

You CAN MAKE BEAUTIFUL BRACELETS by using simple knotting techniques. It does not take long to become an expert, and it is possible to make this craft anywhere, at any time! Wear the bracelets round your wrist or knot them into your hair. Personalize them by using your favourite colors.

SETTING UP

You need different-colored embroidery threads. Knot them together with a 6in (15cm) tassel above the knot. Then secure the knot by a safety pin onto a cushion on your knee. When you become an expert, you may be able to do it with the knot pinned to the knee of your jeans!

WHAT YOU NEED

Two 27.5in (70cm) strands of thread of one color

Two 27.5in (70cm) strands of thread of another color

Safety pin

Cushion

MAKING A BRACELET

1 Knot the threads together (see "setting up".) Spread them out with two same-colored threads on the left and the other two on the right. Lift the left-hand thread and bring it over the one next to it, on the right.

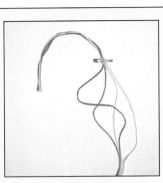

2 Tuck the first thread back underneath and round over the other thread again, making an S shape, as shown. Then slide the first thread up to the top and pull it to make a tight knot. Do these two steps again so you end up with two knots.

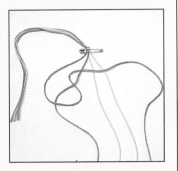

3 Move the thread on the left out of the way and repeat the first two steps using the next two threads along. Repeat for all threads. You will then have made a whole row of knots. Make more rows, starting each time with the thread lying on the left.

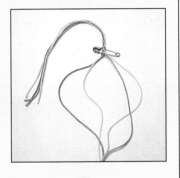

Yellow and blue stripes are a striking combination.

FINISHING OFF

When you get to the end of a striped section, tie all the threads in a knot. Then, unpin the bracelet from the cushion and finish the tassels by braiding or beading them.

The easiest way to complete the tassels is to braid them together, tie them in a knot at the end and trim them near the knot. Put the two middle strands together and braid them as one thread.

If you want, braid the tassels, tie a knot, thread on a large bead and tie another knot to keep it in place. Or leave each tassel free and tie a small bead to the end of each one. Then, place your bracelet on your wrist.

You could hang friendship bracelets in your hair, as well as wearing them on your wrist.

Look for big, bright, wooden beads to use on bracelets.

BRAIDING

Instead of knotting, you could do a simple braided bracelet. Use two threads together as a braiding strand. That way, your bracelet will be thick and bold-looking. Knot the threads as before and pin them to a cushion. Then, always working with the strand on the left, go over, under, over, under the threads to the right.

Don't tighten your knots too much or leave them too loose. You will learn what tension is best by practicing.

Try braiding three, four, five and even six strands. The bracelet will be thicker each time.

Macrame and more

Macrame is the art of tying knots in patterns. It is simple and quick to do, and you can make all kinds of colorful bracelets.

Try making plaited bracelets using colored string, strips of colored braid, or ribbon.

MACRAME BRACELET

This bracelet uses two different-colored sets of threads – four strands of the same color down the middle (the "filler" threads) and two pairs of threads on either side (the "worker" threads), in the second color.

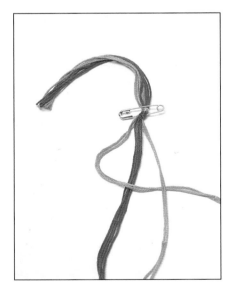

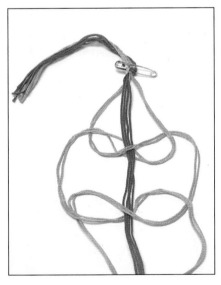

1 *Tie the threads together with a 4in (10cm) tassel and pin the knot on a cushion with the fillers in the middle and the workers either side. Use the pair of workers together, as if they were a single strand. Put the left-hand workers over the fillers and under the right-hand workers.*

2 *Put the right-hand workers under the fillers and over the left-hand workers. Then, pick up the workers which are now on the left and put them under the fillers and over the workers, which are now on the right. Put these right-hand workers up over the fillers and through the loop on the left-hand side, as shown.*

3 *Pull on both sets of workers gently, to tighten the knots you have made. Repeat the process until your bracelet is the length you want. Then, tie all the threads together in a knot and finish the bracelet tassels how you like.*

To tie a bracelet securely, use a reef knot – right end over left end and under, then left end over right end and under.

Make a plain-colored bracelet, using the method on page 18 for stripy bracelets. Then, sew beads onto the bracelet to decorate it.

◀ *Your bracelet will look bright if you use a mixture of colors that contrast well with each other. Do not forget that black and white are a stunning combination, and yellow looks great with blue, green, or red.*

Collage

COLLAGE IS THE ART OF MAKING a picture by putting together lots of different materials because of their interesting colors, shapes, or textures. You can put almost anything on a collage providing you can glue it down successfully.

COLLAGE PICTURE TILE

Mount this miniature picture on a larger mirror tile, or a piece of different-colored card.

WHAT YOU NEED

Square of thick card 5in (12.5cm) x 5in (12.5cm) (for instance, a piece from the side of an empty packing box)
Paint and brushes
Glue, rice, and beans

1 Paint a colorful background on your piece of card. This picture has a green background with yellow spots on.

2 Paint a thick layer of glue all over the inside of the shape. Stick seeds beans, and rice on it to make different-colored areas. Think about using the shapes of the beans. For instance, kidney beans make a good beak on this picture of a rooster.

3 You can add paint as well, if you like. This rooster's tail feathers are made from orange split peas, and beans, which have been painted pink. The body is rice, painted yellow.

Make several different animals on squares of card. Then, display them next to each other.

Here's an unusual valentine, made using beans.

COLLAGE ART

Choose collage materials carefully to get the effect you want. Here are some examples of different styles to try.

Green lentils

Kidney beans

Red lentils

◀ *Stick collage pieces onto a papier mache bowl or pot. This one was covered with a thick layer of glue and then decorated with different-colored beans*

▼ *To brighten up a flower pot, stick buttons and beads all round it.*

▶ *If you break up an eggshell and stick it on a papier mache bowl, it cracks in an interesting way, but won't fall apart.*

▲ *This pot is covered with pieces of eggshell, spray-painted silver.*

Clay jewelry

For centuries, potters have used clay to create works of art. You can do the same using self-hardening clay that does not need to be fired in a kiln. You can then paint and varnish your work to make beautiful things, such as necklaces, bracelets, and badges.

IDEAL GIFTS

Jewelry is easy to make from clay. Make different shapes, such as animals and rainbows. Before the clay hardens, make holes in the shapes for earring fixings or necklace thongs. Or you could tape a safety pin to the back to make a badge.

WHAT YOU NEED

Self-hardening clay

Poster paint and an old tray

Metal jewelry fixings or safety pins

Necklace or string

A POINT TO REMEMBER

Use bright paints to bring the jewelry to life. Add stripes, dots and animal faces.

These badges make great gifts.

Attach your clay shapes to a necklace with jewelry hooks

CLAY HAIR CLIPS

You can make wonderfully shaped clips out of clay, too. You can buy the metal back clip, which is attached with strong glue to the clay front when dry. Make the clay front as thin as possible. But do not worry — it is surprising how light clay is!

Paint and varnish your hair clip when this clay is dry.

▲ *This bracelet is made from beads of clay, with holes made through them with a knitting needle. When dry, the beads are threaded onto the knitting needle and painted or sprayed. Finally, they are threaded on string.*

WHAT YOU NEED

Self-hardening clay
Hair clip
Poster paints and varnish
Strong glue

Buy a plain necklace, as here, or use string or thread.

Use similar shapes for matching necklace and earrings.

Clay crafts

THE BEST SURFACE TO WORK your clay on is a wooden board. You can get different textures on the surface by using the tools listed. If the clay starts to dry out and crack while you are working on it, wet your index finger and smooth over the crack.

WHAT YOU NEED

Self-hardening clay
Candle
Poster paints
Varnish
Modeling tools

CANDLE HOLDER

Fit a candle into a spiral clay candle holder. It would look great on a dinner table.

I Take a large ball of clay and two small balls. Roll the large ball into a long strip and wrap it round the base of the candle. Remove the candle. Make a bottom for the candle holder from another small clay disc.

2 Roll the two small balls into strips of clay. Twist them into a spiral shape. Wet the sides of the base and press the two spirals onto either side, as shown. When dry, paint the candle holder, then varnish it.

MAKING A CLAY POT

It is possible to make lots of different-shaped pots out of self-hardening clay. Paint and varnish them. Then fill them with sweets or pot-pourri to make presents. The best way to begin pot-making is to start with a coil pot. Paint and varnish it when you have finished and the clay is dry.

I Roll out long thin lengths of clay. Wind them in a spiral to form the base of the pot and then the sides.

2 Join new lengths together with wet clay to continue the spiral up to the top. Press gently to make the pot firm.

MIRROR FRAME FROM SELF-HARDENING CLAY

Make a clay mirror frame
and decorate it with stars
and spirals, suns and moons, flowers,
or letter shapes.

WHAT YOU NEED

Poster paint
An old tray
Sponge and rags
Knife
Self-hardening clay
Mirror approx. 4in (9.5cm)
x 5.5in (14cm)

▶ *Paint the frame brightly and varnish it when the paint is dry. Tape a yarn loop to the back so you can hang it up.*

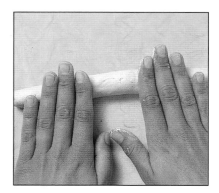

1 *Put a lump of clay on a clean surface such as a tray. Roll your hands over it as shown until it becomes a long evenly-shaped roll. Keep rolling it until it is long enough to go all the way round the edges of your mirror. It should be quite thick all round.*

2 *Carefully lay the roll round the edges of the mirror to form a rectangular frame. Join the roll ends by pushing them together, dabbing on some water and smoothing over the join. Push the roll down to fix it on and make it look flat.*

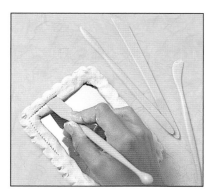

3 *Use clay tools or popsicle sticks to push different shapes and marks into the frame. Make clay shapes such as stars. Put small blobs of wet clay underneath them and push them onto the frame. Allow the finished piece to dry and harden.*

Present wrapping

HERE ARE SOME EASY WAYS TO WRAP and decorate presents so they look almost too good to open!

1 *To cover a square-shaped box, wrap a larger piece of paper round it so that an edge hangs over either end. These edges should measure about half the length of the box. Secure the paper with sticky tape.*

2 *Fold both side edges into the middle in turn, creasing the paper to make them lie flat. The top and bottom edges are now triangle-shaped. Bring them together to meet in the middle, and tape them.*

1 *To cover an oblong-shaped box, fold the paper round it, with an edge hanging over either side. These edges should be as wide as the depth of the box. Tape the paper in place along the box.*

2 *Fold down a top edge so it lies flat. Then, fold in two side edges, creasing the paper so it lies flat. Fold up the bottom edge and turn over the pointed tip to make it neat. Tape it in place.*

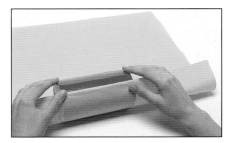  

1 *To wrap a present inside a pretty cracker shape, put the gift inside a cardboard tube. Wrap paper round the tube with the edges hanging over about 4.5in (12cm) at both ends.*

2 *Tape the paper to secure it round the tube. Then, twist the ends and tie them with ribbon, bunching up the wrapping paper. Snip the ends of the cracker into a fringe, or a zigzag line.*

Crepe paper makes good wrapping paper since it is light and easy to fol

WHAT YOU NEED

......

A square of card
6.5in (14cm) x 6.5in (14cm)

Two card rectangles
6.5in (14cm) x 4.5in (10cm)

Compass and pencil

Scissors

Glue

Crayons, felt-tip pens, or paper scraps
to decorate the card

Ruler

Paper fastener

These printing blocks can be used to make the colorful wrapping paper, shown below

PERSONALIZED PAPER

To make your own unique wrapping paper, buy some plain-colored sheets. Then, cut out some squares of card for printing blocks. Stick string on the card in shapes, such as flowers, fish or hearts. When dry, dab poster paint onto the string and press them down firmly over the wrapping paper. You will need to keep adding more paint so that each printed shape is bright and sharp.

Add two or more printed shapes to one piece of paper.

Making mobiles

A MOBILE IS A MOVING SCULPTURE where hanging objects are carefully balanced from a frame. So long as they are correctly balanced you can use almost any object — but remember to think about what they will look like when viewed from underneath and from all sides.

SPIRAL MOBILE

Try this easy mobile to start with. It is based on a spiral made from colored card.

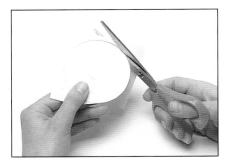

1 *Cut a spiral from the card circle and make four holes along the length. Paint and cut out four shapes of about the same size. Make a hole in the top of each one.*

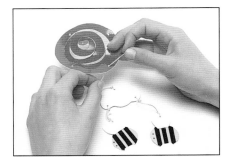

2 *Push a length of thread through each hole and knot the end to secure it. Knot the other ends through the holes in the spiral. Hang the mobile up with thread.*

Hang smaller shapes from the larger ones, experimenting to get the right balance.

NATURAL MOBILE

Find natural objects, such as shells and pebbles, to hang from a mobile. This mobile is made from a starfish shell, but you could get a similar effect using a coathanger.

Begin by covering a coathanger with pretty strips of material. Then, either make holes in the shells with a needle and push through the thread, or simply tie the thread around the shells. You could also use buttons and beads. Then hang everything from the coathanger.

WHAT YOU NEED

Natural objects,
such as shells and pebbles
Beads and buttons
Strong thread
Needle
Coathanger
Pretty rags

◀ *This mobile works because the starfish shape is symmetrical, which means its shape is balanced all round. See if you can think of other symmetrical shapes you could use for the main part of a mobile!*

Hang small, light objects near the top of the thread, and large, heavy ones at the bottom.

SPACE MOBILE

This outer-space mobile glints and glitters in the light! The objects hang from a thick cardboard star shape, covered with silver foil. Don't forget to balance the objects so the mobile hangs evenly from the ceiling!

The planets are made from painted polystyrene balls – cut one ball in half to make martians!

Make a spaceship from a toilet-roll tube, covering it with silver foil, or painting it.

You could use silver thread to complete the shiny effect.

WHAT YOU NEED

Thick card

Polystyrene balls

toilet-roll tube

Glue

Silver foil

Glitter

Paint

Brush

Silver or black thread

Scissors

Tiny bells (optional)

Stars and moons can be cut out from card and painted.

◀ *Your space mobile will jangle in the breeze if you can find some tiny bells to hang on it.*

Tiny bell

ADDING EXTRA SPARKLE
Dab on glue to add glitter to the space objects.